What's it all a

Relationships are e
important aspect
with our parents, bo, ... or girlfriend, husband
or wife, children, grandchildren, friends, and so on.

Christianity is first and foremost about relationships
rather than rules. It is about a Person more than
a philosophy. It is about the most important
relationship of all: our relationship with the God
who made us. Jesus said that the first and greatest
commandment is to love God. The second is to love
our neighbour. So, it is also about our relationships
with other people.

3

Why do we need him?

You and I were created to live in a relationship with God. Until we find that relationship there will always

be something missing in our lives. As a result, we are often aware of a gap. One rock singer described it by saying: 'I've got an emptiness deep inside.'

A woman, in a letter to me, wrote of 'a deep deep void'. Another young girl spoke of 'a chunk missing in her soul'.

People try to fill this emptiness in various ways.

Some try to close the gap with money, but that does not satisfy. Aristotle Onassis, who was one of the richest men in the world, said at the end of his life: 'Millions do not always add up to what a man needs out of life.'

Why Jesus?

Nicky Gumbel

Illustrated by
Charlie Mackesy

Copyright © Nicky Gumbel

The right of Nicky Gumbel to be identified as author of this work has been asserted by him in accordance with the Copyright, Designs and Patents Act 1988.

First published by Kingsway Publications Ltd in 1991.
First published by Alpha International 1997.

This edition published by Alpha International in 2023.
10 9 8 7 6 5 4 3 2 1

All rights reserved. No part of this guide or any other Alpha publication may be reproduced or transmitted in any form or by any means, electronic or mechanical, including photocopy, recording or any information storage and retrieval system, without permission in writing from the copyright holder or the expressly authorised agent thereof. Where an Alpha publication is offered free of charge the fee is waived on condition the publication is used to run or promote Alpha and should not be subject to any subsequent fee or charge. This resource may not be modified or used for any commercial purpose without permission in writing from the copyright holder or the expressly authorised agent thereof.

ISBN 978 1 912263 89 9

Scripture quotations taken from the Holy Bible, New International Version Anglicised. Copyright © 1979, 1984, 2011 Biblica, formerly International Bible Society. Used by permission of Hodder & Stoughton Publishers, an Hachette UK company. All rights reserved. 'NIV' is a registered trademark of Biblica. UK trademark number 1448790.

Published by Alpha International,
HTB Brompton Road, London, SW7 1JA.

Email: ukpublishing@alpha.org
Website: alpha.org
@alphacourse

Illustrations by Charlie Mackesy

Others try drugs or excess alcohol or sexual promiscuity. One woman said to me, 'These things provide instant gratification but they leave you feeling hollow afterwards.' Still others try hard work, music, sport or seek success. There may not be anything wrong with these in themselves but they do not satisfy that hunger deep inside every human being.

Even the closest human relationships, wonderful though they are, do not in themselves satisfy this 'emptiness deep inside'.

Nothing will fill this gap except the relationship with God for which we were made.

According to the New Testament, the reason for this emptiness is that men and women have turned their backs on God.

Jesus said, 'I am the bread of life' (John 6:35). He is the only one who can satisfy our deepest hunger because he is the one who makes it possible for our relationship with God to be restored.

a) He satisfies our hunger for meaning and purpose in life

At some point everyone asks the question, 'What am I doing on earth?' or, 'What is the point of life?' or, 'Is there any purpose to life?'. As Albert Camus once said, 'Man cannot live without meaning.'

Until we are living in a relationship with God we will never find the true meaning and purpose of life. Other things may provide passing satisfaction but it does not last. Only in a relationship with our Creator do we find the true meaning and purpose of our lives.

b) He satisfies our hunger for life beyond death

Before I was a Christian I did not like to think about the subject of death. My own death seemed a long way in the future. I did not know what would happen and I did not want to think about it. I was failing to face up to reality. The fact is that we will all die. Yet God has 'set eternity in the human heart' (Ecclesiastes 3:11). Most people do not want to die. We long to survive beyond death. Only in Jesus Christ do we find eternal life. For our relationship with God, which starts now, survives death and goes on into eternity.

c) He satisfies our hunger for forgiveness

If we are honest, we would have to admit that we all do things that we know are wrong. Sometimes we do things of which we are deeply ashamed. More than that, there is a self-centredness about our lives which spoils them. Jesus said, 'What comes out of you is what makes you "unclean". For from within, out of your hearts, come evil thoughts, sexual immorality, theft, murder, adultery, greed, malice, deceit, lewdness, envy, slander, arrogance and folly. All these evils come from inside and make you "unclean"' (Mark 7:20–23).

Our greatest need, in fact, is for forgiveness. Just as someone who has cancer needs a doctor whether they realise it or not, so we need forgiveness whether we realise it or not. Just as with cancer, those who recognise their need are far better off than those who are lulled into a false sense of security.

By his death on the cross, Jesus made it possible for us to be forgiven and brought back into a relationship with God. In this way, he supplied the answer to our deepest need.

Why bother with Jesus?

Why should we bother with Christianity? The simple answer is because it is true. If Christianity is not true, we are wasting our time. If it is true, then it must be of vital importance to every human being.

But how do we know it is true?

We can test the claims of Christianity because it is an historical faith. It is based on the life, death and resurrection of Jesus Christ. Our faith is based on firm historical evidence.

Who is Jesus?

Jesus is the most remarkable man who ever lived. He is the centrepiece of our civilisation. After all, we call what happened before him 'BC' and what happened after him 'AD'.

Jesus was and is the Son of God. Some people think he is just a 'good religious teacher'.

However, that suggestion does not fit with the facts.

a) His claims

Jesus claimed to be the unique Son of God – on an equal footing with God. He assumed the authority to forgive sins. He said that one day he would judge the world and that what would matter then would be how we had responded to him in this life.

C. S. Lewis pointed out that: 'A man who was merely a man and said the sort of things Jesus said would not be a great moral teacher.' He would either be insane or else he would be 'the Devil of Hell'. 'You must make your choice,' he writes. Either Jesus was, and is, the Son of God or else he was insane or evil but, C. S. Lewis goes on, 'let us not come up with any patronising nonsense about his being a great human teacher. He has not left that open to us. He did not intend to.'[1]

b) His character

Many people who do not profess to be Christians regard Jesus as the supreme example of a selfless life. Dostoevsky, himself a Christian, said, 'I believe there is no one lovelier, deeper, more sympathetic and more perfect than Jesus. I say to myself, with jealous love, that not only is there no one else like him but there could never be anyone like him.'

As far as his teaching is concerned, there seems to be general agreement that it is the purest and best ever to have fallen from human lips.

To C. S. Lewis it seemed clear that he could neither have been insane or evil and thus he concludes, 'however strange or terrifying or unlikely it may seem, I have to accept the view that he was and is God.'

c) His conquest of death

The evidence for the physical resurrection is very strong indeed. When the disciples went to the tomb, they found that the grave clothes had collapsed and that Jesus' body was absent.

In the next six weeks, he was seen by over 500 people. The disciples' lives were transformed and the Christian church was born, and then grew at a dynamic rate.

A former Lord Chief Justice of England, Lord Darling, said of the resurrection: 'In its favour as living truth there exists such overwhelming evidence, positive and negative, factual and circumstantial, that no intelligent jury in the world could fail to

bring in a verdict that the resurrection story is true.'
The only satisfactory explanation for these facts is
that Jesus did indeed rise from the dead and thus
confirms that he was, and is, the Son of God.

Why did he come?

Jesus is the only man who has ever chosen to be
born, and he is one of the few who has chosen to
die. He said that the entire reason for his coming
was to die for us. He came 'to give his life as a
ransom for many' (Mark 10:45).

From what we know of crucifixion, it was one of
the cruellest forms of execution. Cicero described
it as 'the most cruel and hideous of tortures'. Jesus
would have been flogged with a whip of several
strands of leather weighted with pieces of metal
and bones. According to Eusebius, a third-century
historian, 'The sufferer's veins were laid bare, and the
very muscles, sinews and bowels of the victim were
opened to exposure.'

Jesus was then forced to carry a six-foot cross
beam until he collapsed. When he reached the site
of execution, six-inch nails were hammered through
his wrists and feet as he was nailed to the cross. He
was left to hang for hours in excruciating pain.

Yet, the New Testament makes it clear that there
was something worse for Jesus than the physical
and emotional pain; this was the spiritual anguish of
being separated from God as he carried all our sins.

Why did he die?

Jesus said he died 'for' us. The word 'for' means 'instead of'. He did it because he loved us and did not want us to have to pay the penalty for all the things that we had done wrong. On the cross he was effectively saying, 'I will take all those things on myself.' He did it for you and he did it for me. If you or I had been the only person in the world he would have done it for us. St Paul wrote of 'the Son of God, who loved me and gave himself for me' (Galatians 2:20). It was out of love for us that he gave his life as a ransom.

The word 'ransom' comes from the slave market. A kind person might buy a slave to set him free – but first the ransom price had to be paid. Jesus paid, by his blood on the cross, the ransom price to set us free.

Freedom from what?

a) Freedom from guilt

Whether we feel guilty or not, we are all guilty before God because of the many times we have broken his laws in thought, word and deed. Just as when someone commits a crime there is a penalty to be paid, in the same way there is a penalty for breaking God's law. 'The wages of sin is death' (Romans 6:23).

The result of the things we do wrong is being cut off to spiritual death – being cut off from God eternally. We all deserve to suffer that penalty. On the cross, Jesus took the penalty in our place so that we could be totally forgiven and our guilt could be taken away.

b) Freedom from addiction

Jesus said that 'everyone who sins is a slave to sin' (John 8:34). Jesus died to set us free from that slavery. On the cross, the power of this addiction was broken. Although we may still fall from time to time, the power of this addiction is broken when Jesus sets us free. That is why Jesus went on to say that 'if the Son sets you free, you will be free indeed' (John 8:36).

c) Freedom from fear

Jesus came so that 'by his death he might destroy him who holds the power of death – that is, the devil – and free those who all their lives were held in slavery by their fear of death' (Hebrews 2:14–15). We need no longer fear death.

Death is not the end for those whom Jesus has set free. Rather it is the gateway to heaven, where we will be free from even the presence of sin. When Jesus set us free from the fear of death, he also set us free from all other fears.

Freedom for what?

Jesus is no longer physically on earth, but he has not left us alone. He has sent his Holy Spirit to be with us. When his Spirit comes to live within us, he gives us a new freedom.

a) Freedom to know God

The things that we do wrong cause a barrier between us and God: 'your iniquities have separated you from your God' (Isaiah 59:2). When Jesus died on the cross, he removed the barrier that existed between us and God. As a result he has made it possible for us to have a relationship with our Creator. We become his sons and daughters. The Spirit assures us of this relationship, and he helps us to get to know God better. He helps us to pray and to understand God's word (the Bible).

b) Freedom to love

'We love because he first loved us' (1 John 4:19). As we look at the cross, we understand God's love for us. When the Spirit of God comes to live within us, we experience that love. As we do so, we receive a new love for God and for other people. We are set free to live a life of love – a life centred around loving and serving Jesus and loving and serving other people rather than a life centred around ourselves.

c) Freedom to change

People sometimes say, 'You are what you are. You can't change.' The good news is that with the help of the Spirit we can change. The Holy Spirit gives us the freedom to live the sort of lives that deep down we have always wanted to live. St Paul tells us that the fruit of the Spirit is 'love, joy, peace, patience, kindness, goodness, faithfulness, gentleness and self-control' (Galatians 5:22–23). When we ask the Spirit of God to come and live within us, these wonderful characteristics begin to grow in our lives.

Why not?

So God offers us in Christ Jesus forgiveness, freedom and his Spirit to live within us. All this is a gift from God. When someone offers us a present, we have a choice. We can either accept it, open it and enjoy it. Or else we can say, 'No thank you.' Sadly, many people make excuses for not accepting the gift that God offers.

Here are some of the excuses:

a) 'I have no need of God'

When people say this they usually mean that they are quite happy without God. What they fail to realise is that our greatest need is not 'happiness' but 'forgiveness'. It takes a very proud person to say that they have no need of forgiveness.

We all need forgiveness. Without it, we are in serious trouble. For God is not only our loving Father; he is also a righteous judge.

Either we accept what Jesus has done for us on the cross, or else one day we will pay the just penalty ourselves for the things we have done wrong.

b) 'There is too much to give up'

Sometimes, God puts his finger on something in our lives which we know is wrong and which we would have to give up if we want to enjoy this relationship with God through Jesus.

But we need to remember:

- God loves us. He asks us only to give up things that do us harm. If my children were playing with a carving knife, I would tell them to stop, not because I want to ruin their fun but because I do not want them to get hurt.

- What we give up is nothing compared to what we receive. The cost of not becoming a Christian is far greater than the cost of becoming a Christian.

- What we give up is nothing compared to what Jesus gave up when he died on the cross for us.

c) 'There must be a trap'

Understandably, people often find it hard to accept that there is anything free in this life. They think it all sounds too easy and that there must be some hidden trap. However, what they fail to realise is that although it is free for us, it was not free for Jesus. He paid for it with his own blood. It is easy for us but it was not easy for him.

d) 'I'm not good enough'

None of us is good enough. Nor can we ever make

ourselves good enough for God. But that is why Jesus came. He made it possible for God to accept us just as we are, whatever we have done and however much of a mess we have made of our lives.

e) 'I could never keep it up'

We are right to think that we could never keep it up. We cannot by ourselves, but the Spirit of God, who comes to live within us, gives us the power and the strength to keep going as Christians.

f) 'I'll do it later'

This is perhaps the most common excuse. Sometimes people say, 'I know it's true, but I'm not ready.' They put it off. The longer we put it off the harder it becomes and the more we miss out. We never know whether we will get another opportunity. Speaking for myself, my only regret is that I did not accept the gift earlier.

What do we have to do?

The New Testament makes it clear that we have to do something to accept the gift that God offers. This is an act of faith. John writes that 'God so loved the world that he gave his one and only Son, that whoever believes in him shall not perish but have eternal life' (John 3:16). Believing involves an act of faith, based on all that we know about Jesus. It is not blind faith. It is putting our trust in a Person. In some ways, it is like the step of faith taken by a bride or a bridegroom when they say, 'I will' on their wedding day.

The way people take this step of faith varies enormously, but I want to describe one way in which you can take this step of faith right now. It can be summarised by three very simple words:

a) 'Sorry'

You have to ask God to forgive you for all the things you have done wrong and turn from everything which you know is wrong in your life. This is what the Bible means by 'repentance'.

b) 'Thank you'

We believe that Jesus died for us on the cross. You need to thank him for dying for you and for the offer of his free gift of forgiveness, freedom and his Spirit.

c) 'Please'

God never forces his way into our lives. You need to accept his gift and invite him to come and live within you by his Spirit.

If you would like to have a relationship with God and you are ready to say these three things, then here is a very simple prayer which you can pray and which will be the start of that relationship:

Lord Jesus Christ,

I am sorry for the things I have done wrong in my life (take a few moments to ask his forgiveness for anything particular that is on your conscience). Please forgive me. I now turn from everything which I know is wrong.

Thank you that you died on the cross for me so that I could be forgiven and set free.

Thank you that you offer me forgiveness and the gift of your Spirit. I now receive that gift.

Please come into my life by your Holy Spirit to be with me forever.

Thank you, Lord Jesus.

Amen.

What now?

1. Tell someone

It is important to tell someone in order to underline the decision you have made. Often it is only when you tell someone else that it becomes a reality to you. It is probably best to start by telling someone who you think will be pleased to hear the news.

2. Read the Bible

Once we have received Jesus and put our trust in him, we become children of God (John 1:12). He is our heavenly Father. Like any father, he wants us to have a close relationship with him. We develop this relationship as we listen to him (primarily through the Bible) and as we speak to him in prayer. The Bible is the word of God and you might find it helpful to begin by reading a few verses of John's Gospel every day. Ask God to speak to you as you read.

3. Start to speak to God each day (i.e. pray)

I find the following a great help:

A - Adoration
Praising God for who he is and what he has done.

C – Confession

Asking God's forgiveness for anything that we have done wrong.

T – Thanksgiving

Thanking God for health, family, friends and so on.

S – Supplication

Praying for ourselves, for our friends and for others.

4. Join a lively church

It is important to be part of a group of Christians who get together to worship God, to hear what God is saying to them, to encourage one another and to make friends. Church should be an exciting place!

I first prayed a prayer like the one on page 20 on 16 February 1974. It changed my life. It is the best and most important thing I have ever done. I trust it will be the same for you.

Further reading:

Questions of Life by Nicky Gumbel, which looks in greater detail at the relevance of Jesus to our lives today and explores the basics of the Christian faith.

30 Days by Nicky Gumbel, is a practical introduction to reading the Bible. Whether you've been a Christian for years, but find reading Scripture a struggle, or you're exploring faith for the first time, *30 Days* will help you start reading the Bible in an easy and accessible way.

Notes:

[1] *Mere Christianity* by CS Lewis © CS Lewis Pte Ltd 1942, 1943, 1944, 1952.

Try Alpha

Alpha is a series of
interactive sessions that
explore the Christian faith

Each talk looks at a different question
around life, faith and meaning, and is
designed to spark discussion.

Alpha runs in cafés, churches, homes,
and even online. Each session has three
key elements: a time to connect, a talk,
and space for good conversation.

Find out more
about Alpha at:

alpha.org.uk

To purchase
Alpha resources,
head to:

shop.alpha.org